Madge and Lou Lou

Madge and Lou Lou

Written and Illustrated By Angie Crouch

Each morning the rooster crows to wake up Madge and Lou Lou. Can you crow to wake them up?

Cock-a -doodle -doo!

Howdy Lou Lou!
We have a hankern'
for your eggs!

Yes, I can!

Are the eggs

of

on top of   the cow?

Are the eggs above the pig?

Are the eggs beside the sheep?

Are the eggs under the horse?

Are the eggs inside

the snake?

Hold your horses varmint! No one steals my eggs!

Lou Lou was so mad that she decided to kick the snake right off the farm!

Thank you for helping us find Lou Lou's eggs. We won't have to worry about that snake ever again! Bless his little heart!

ISBN-13: 978-0692054895
ISBN-10: 0692054898

ALABAMA

This book is dedicated to my first best friend, my brother, Dominic Stremel. Nick, you were the best little buddy ever! I still feel bad for leaving you in the tree of yellow jackets and for snagging your foot with my fishing hook. I hope that our own children will experience running around barefoot while catching fireflies at night! ~Angelina

About the Author

Angie Crouch was born in Hugoton, Kansas. She spent her childhood years on her family farm near Hanceville, Alabama and Hartford, Kansas. She has been an early childhood educator for fourteen years. Angie and her husband share their home in Lexington, South Carolina with their two amazing daughters.

www.ingramcontent.com/pod-product-compliance
Lightning Source LLC
Chambersburg PA
CBHW041241040426
42445CB00004B/105